Drawing Made Easy

SHORTCUTS
& ARTISTS' SECRETS

By Diane Cardaci

www.walterfoster.com

This library edition published in 2013 by Walter Foster Publishing, Inc.
Walter Foster Library
3 Wrigley, Suite A, Irvine, CA 92618

Printed in Mankato, Minnesota, USA by CG Book Printers, a division of Corporate Graphics.

First Library Edition

Library of Congress Cataloging-in-Publication Data

Cardaci, Diane.
  Shortcuts & artists' secrets / by Diane Cardaci.
    pages cm. -- (Drawing made easy)
  Includes bibliographical references.
1. Pencil drawing--Technique. I. Title. II. Title: Shortcuts and artists' secrets.
  NC890.C37 2013
  741.2--dc23
                                                  2013011656

052013
18134

9 8 7 6 5 4 3 2 1

TABLE OF CONTENTS

INTRODUCTION

One of the great bonuses of learning to draw is that it slows us down and is a great antidote for the fast paced, hi-tech world of the 21st century. One of the most important keys to our growth as an artist is patience—not only for improving our skills, but also patience in executing a drawing. It is no quick task to do artwork using such a small tool as a pencil. If we try to speed things up too much, we often find ourselves frustrated that our drawing does not have the quality that we are striving for. However, there are some simple things that we can do to help save time while we draw.

Over the years, there have been many artists who have kindly shared their tricks of the trade with me. Also, through experimentation, I have developed some of my own timesaving techniques. In this book, I would like to pass on to you some of my favorite and most useful tips that help speed things along. Try working with these and see how you enjoy them. But I also hope that you will experiment and find some of your own unique ways of working.

TOOLS AND MATERIALS

You don't need much to draw—just a few simple basics. These are some of my favorite tools and materials, but you can experiment with what you like and find some favorites of your own too.

Pencils

Intricate or detailed drawings call for harder leads, or H pencils. These hard pencils are labeled 9H to H, with the highest number being the hardest. Soft pencils run from B to 9B, with the 9B being the softest. These pencils create much darker lines and velvety tones. You can also choose graphite lead holders that come in different diameters, or woodless pencils, which have the advantage of a larger diameter lead.

Sharpeners

If you choose a traditional pencil, you will also need a sharpener. You can choose from small, portable handheld sharpeners as well as electric sharpeners. To sharpen the leads in a lead holder, you will need a specialized sharpener that is called a pointer.

Erasers

My favorite eraser is the kneaded eraser. It can be molded much like a piece of clay, so you have a lot of control over what you want to erase. There are also vinyl erasers as well as electric erasers. It is also very handy to have an erasing shield, which works like a stencil and protects other parts of the drawing.

Using a Sandpaper Block

Although it is easiest to sharpen your pencil with a handheld or electric pencil sharpener, there may be times when you need to slow down and manually sharpen your pencil. You would want to do this when you would like to create a specialized point, or because the pencil does not fit into a mechanical sharpener (such as a carpenter's pencil or large lead pencil).

First use a utility knife to whittle down the wood part of the pencil.

Use a sandpaper block to sand down the lead into a point.

PAPERS

Using Paper to Your Advantage

Choosing the right kind of paper for your drawing can actually save you time in the long run. Smooth paper, such as plate finish or hot pressed, is perfect for creating very detailed drawings. On the other hand, if you would like to have a lot of texture in your drawing, it is much easier to use a paper that has some "tooth," or texture. Textured paper, such as cold pressed, does the work for you in creating texture. Rough watercolor paper gives you even more texture to work with. The raised areas of rough paper pick up the graphite of your pencil easily, while the lower areas do not. Once you experiment with different paper types, you'll see how you can use the smooth and rough textures to help you create your drawing.

Choosing Paper

Here you can see how the same pencil (3B) looks on five different types of paper. It's a good idea to experiment with papers on your own too, so you can see how you can use the paper texture to your advantage in a drawing.

Plate finish Bristol paper

Vellum Bristol paper

Smooth watercolor paper

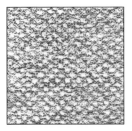

Regular watercolor paper

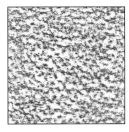

Rough watercolor paper

YOUR STUDIO

Setting Up Your Studio

▶ It is not necessary to have a fancy studio to create great artwork—many artists work at their kitchen table or in their living room. For years, I worked on a drawing board leaned against a table. But if you are able to have a separate studio space, you will want a drawing table or easel, a cart or taboret for your supplies, and adequate lighting. I prefer to work standing up, but when I do sit, I use a studio chair that provides good back support. I have much of my studio equipment on wheels so I can move it around if I need to, and my easel, although sturdy enough for a large drawing or painting, is lightweight enough that I can bring it outdoors to work in my garden on a beautiful summer day.

It's Easy to Carry Your Studio With You

◀ Whenever you go out, make it a habit to "bring your studio" with you. Great artists have always spent many hours drawing outside of their studios—at cafés, train stations, public gardens, or virtually anywhere. Sketching everywhere and every day is one of the fastest ways to hone your drawing skills. All you really need to sketch when you're out is a sketchbook, a couple of pencils, a sharpener, and a kneaded eraser.

Easels and supports

It is always better (and easier!) to draw with your paper vertically or at a comfortable angle. Drawing flat on a table can introduce distortions to your work. Also, by looking at your drawing straight on using an easel or support, it's easier to see where you need to improve your drawing.

▶ A table easel, such as this one, is a small easel that is perfect if you have limited space. Drawing boards are another great option if you're looking for portability. You can also use a standard easel, which can range from very lightweight and portable to more heavy, large versions that are meant for studio use.

MAKING THE PENCIL DO THE WORK

Choosing The Right Pencil For The Job

If you're working on a drawing that has a good amount of detail, remember that you'll save some time by working with hard pencils. For the detail work in my drawings, I usually use an HB and sometimes a 2H. But if you want plenty of dark, rich tones and detail is not as crucial, soft pencils are the best choice. Also, by changing the pressure, soft pencils can show greater variety in the strokes.

◄ On the far left, strokes were created with a 5H pencil, which has a hard lead. On the immediate left, strokes were created with a 6B pencil, which has a much softer lead. You can see how the strokes of the 5H pencil are much sharper.

Using The Side of the Pencil

► When drawing, practice creating strokes with the side of your pencil. Here, I used a 3B pencil in both strokes, but I used the side of the pencil at the right and the point of the pencil on the left. You can see how using the side of the pencil creates a much wider stroke, which is helpful for shading or covering more area of the paper quickly.

2B	B	HB	H	2H

Holding the Pencil

Try holding the pencil in different ways to see how it affects your drawing. Some positions are better for detail work, while others are better for larger strokes.

The most common position is the writing position; this is best for detail work because it involves using the small, fine muscles of your hand.

The underhand position is good for when you're using the side of the pencil. Holding the pencil this way uses more of your arm muscles, so it is also good for long, free strokes.

The overhand position is an alternative for creating long, free strokes.

Quick and Easy—One Pencil, Many Jobs

By using a moderately soft pencil, you can achieve a variety of effects in your drawing. These strokes were all created with the same 3B pencil. Experiment with these techniques, and then see if you can find some other new ways of using your pencil as well.

Change the pressure as you draw to give your lines energy and interest.

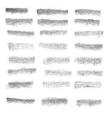

Use the side of the pencil to draw a pattern with straight, short lines for a shortcut to drawing bricks or patterns.

Use the point of the pencil to scribble in bushes or trees.

Scribble with the side of the pencil to indicate softer, darker foliage.

Use the side of the pencil to scribble in the darker, softer tones, and then use the point of the pencil for details in shrubbery.

For a quickly rendered brick or stone wall, combine short horizontal strokes with the side of the pencil with detailed strokes from the point.

WORKING WITH TRACING PAPER

I always keep plenty of tracing paper in my studio, as it can be a big help in speeding up your drawing. Tracing paper comes in two weights—the heavyweight paper is often called tracing vellum and can withstand a lot of erasing, so it is a great help for developing a drawing. I use the lightweight tracing paper mainly to protect the drawing.

Developing a Drawing: Tomatoes

When you work on a freehand drawing, tracing paper helps you develop the details. The way to do this is to begin a drawing using some basic lines and shapes. Then lay a piece of tracing paper over this to develop the drawing using   lines underneath as guides. You can continue to do this, using a new piece of tracing paper every time you want to refine the drawing further.

First block in the main shapes of your subject.

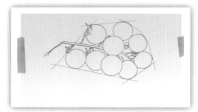

Then tape a piece of tracing paper over your drawing and redraw the smaller shapes.

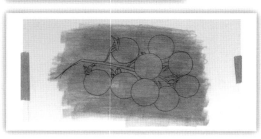

◀ Next smear graphite over the back of the drawing with a soft pencil. Use some tissue to smear the graphite and make it an even layer. Then tape the drawing to a new piece of paper and redraw the lines with a sharp, hard pencil to transfer the graphite onto your paper. Use just enough pressure make the graphite transfer, but not so much that the pencil makes an impression in the paper.

▶ Remove the tracing paper and clean up any smudges on the drawing paper with a kneaded eraser.

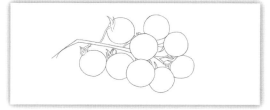

Other Uses For Tracing Paper:

- Composition: Sometimes when you are working on a drawing, you may want to change or add an element, but you are not exactly sure where you want to place it. If you draw it on a separate piece of tracing paper, you can move it around to see where you want it.
- Protection: When you have finished a drawing, cover it with tracing paper to protect it from dust and smearing until you are ready to frame it.
- Masking: Cut shapes out of heavyweight tracing paper and use them to "mask" selected areas of your work while you are drawing.

Tip!

As you work, always keep a piece of tracing paper under your hand so that your hand does not smear the drawing.

EASY WAYS TO SEE VALUES

Values are the lightness or darkness of the subject—when you look at a black and white photograph you are seeing only the values and not the hues (the colors) of your subject. It can be very confusing to learn to evaluate values, but here are three simple tricks you can use to help.

Squint   When as you look at objects, make a habit of squinting and comparing the lightness and darkness that you see to a value scale. Squinting cuts down on the light entering your eyes, so the color is not so distracting.

Black and White If you're working from a photograph, you can make a black-and-white copy of it to help you see the values. If you are working from life, you can take a black-and-white photo of your subject and refer to it while you are working.

Thumbnail Value Sketches Thumbnail sketches are small sketches that simplify values. Because you're working on such a small scale, you're forced to look for the big value patterns in your subject. When creating a thumbnail sketch, try to simplify the values into no more than five values. It is helpful to think of the large value shapes almost as pieces of a puzzle. Spend no more than 5-10 minutes on a thumbnail sketch—this will help you learn to quickly evaluate values.

11

MEASURING PROPORTIONS

Getting the right proportions in your drawing can be challenging, but there is a very simple trick you can use to get them right.

When studying your subject, place your arm out directly from your shoulder. Then when you want to measure the height of something (for example, the height of a tree), line up the tip of your pencil with the top of what you want to measure, and then move your thumb to measure the distance of the height. You now have a measurement that you can use to compare with other parts of the subject. You can even turn your hand horizontally to compare the height to the width.

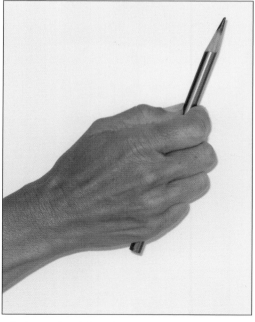

When you measure, it's important to remember to keep your pencil perfectly vertical, and also to keep your arm straight out from your shoulder without bending your elbow. This can be seen in the photo above at left. In the photo above at right, you can see two common errors—my arm is not horizontal and the pencil is not vertical.

Sight Sizing: A Simple Way To Study Proportions

Proportion isn't the only important part of a drawing; sometimes you also have to enlarge or reduce your subject. For example, when you measure a setup for a still life drawing, you may find that it is either too small or too large for the paper when you put the measurements down.

Some artists like to use a method that helps overcome this difficulty, which is called the "sight size" method of drawing. In the sight size method, you draw your subject exactly the same size as what you are viewing. To do this, adjust the position of the easel in relation to your subject so that when you take your measurements, you can copy them exactly. This method works best for subjects such as portraits and still lifes.

Here I positioned the vase with flowers so that it "fits" on the paper. When I take my measurements, I can place those measurements directly on the paper.

Here I moved the vase closer to the easel. As a result, if I draw the exact measurements as I see them, my subject will be too big for the paper.

QUICK WAYS TO BLEND

Blending value changes is an important skill to develop in drawing. It is a good idea to experiment with different techniques and find the ones that you are most comfortable with.

There are two different approaches to creating blended effects with tools in your drawing. A common technique is to place tone on your paper with the side of your pencil, and then smear it with a blending tool. Another approach is to use graphite or charcoal powder to smear on your paper. You can either purchase the powder at an art supply store, or you can collect shavings from your pencils in a cup to use as the powder. Dip your blending tool into the graphite or charcoal, and smear it on your paper. It takes a bit of practice and experimentation at first, but once you develop a feel for it, your drawing process will go much faster.

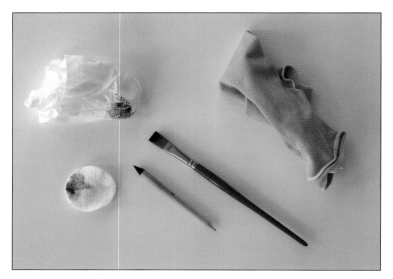

Blending With Tools There are many tools that can be used to blend, and some of them can be found around the house: facial tissues, rags, a paintbrush, blending stump, and a cotton pad are all tools I use to blend. The stump (or tortillon) is one of my favorite tools for blending delicate areas because it has a point. Stumps can be purchased at art stores and come in a variety of sizes. For blending large areas, I prefer to use a rag or chamois cloth.

Pencil Strokes Blended with Stump I put down a layer of horizontal pencil strokes, using heavier pressure on the left side, and then blended with a stump.

Graphite Powder with Stump Here I dipped the stump in graphite powder and started my strokes on the left, stroking toward the right.

Charcoal Pencil Strokes Blended with Stump I used a charcoal pencil to create horizontal strokes, again using heavier pressure on the left side and blending with a stump.

Charcoal Powder with Stump Here I dipped the stump in charcoal powder and started on the left, dragging the stump toward the right.

Blending Without Tools

For most of my more delicate drawings, I do not use tools to blend—I find that using just the pencil is a more sensitive approach. Other times, I will only use a blending tool at the end of drawing. It does take more practice and control to blend values without tools, but the results are well worth the effort. One of the best exercises to develop this control is to practice making swatches until you have the techniques down pat.

The best way to get even tones is by using either hatching or crosshatching strokes. Hatching strokes are parallel lines, whereas crosshatching strokes are parallel lines that change direction and cross the previous strokes.

Creating Blended Tones with Hatching Using the side of my pencil, I used long, parallel horizontal strokes, adding pressure while stroking to the right to create darker tone.

Here, I followed the same process as above, but I used curved parallel strokes to build up the tone. This would be a good technique to use for a curved subject.

Creating Blended Tones with Crosshatching Here I first used horizontal parallel strokes to cover the area. Then I changed directions, using parallel diagonal strokes. This gives a denser coverage and blend.

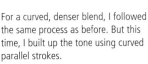

For a curved, denser blend, I followed the same process as before. But this time, I built up the tone using curved parallel strokes.

When you want a really smooth tone, use a harder pencil over a layer of softer pencil. For example, for a dark tone, start with a 6B, and then go over it with a 2B or HB. The harder pencil pushes some of the graphite into the valleys of the textured paper.

Tip!

SECRETS TO CREATIVITY

The fastest way to improve your drawing skills is to develop two essential habits. If you do, I can promise that you will soon be amazed at the progress you are making in your drawings. In addition, these habits will inspire you and stretch your "creativity muscles."

1. Sketch Every Day Sketching not only develops your hand-eye coordination, but it's also a wonderful way to connect with the visual world around you. Carry your sketchbook around with you everywhere, and draw as many different types of subjects as possible. You will soon find yourself getting inspired and will have many ideas for drawings from your sketchbooks.

2. Sketch from Old Masters' Work The Old Masters were thoroughly trained in their craft, and their drawings contain knowledge that can be absorbed when you copy them. It is great to do quick sketches of their work to get a sense of the composition of their drawings. And don't be afraid to use one of their compositional ideas—great artists have copied compositions from other great artists for centuries!

Some other tips for inspiring your creativity are:

• ***Keep a Picture Collection*** *Collect pictures of subjects that interest you. Build up your collection over time, and it will become an invaluable resource.*

• ***Always Carry a Camera*** *You never know when you will spot something of interest and won't have time to sit down and sketch it on the spot.*

• ***Go to Museums*** *We are lucky to live in an age where, even if we don't live in a big city with great museums, we can take a virtual trip to a museum on the Internet. Most of the world's greatest museums now have websites where you can visit their collections online. Viewing famous works of art will keep you inspired!*

SPEED SKETCHING

So often, we feel that we don't have the time to take out our sketchbooks to draw. But even if you only have five minutes, you can benefit from doing what I like to call "speed sketching." The idea is to quickly put down the big shapes, lines, and angles of your subject, which are the armature of any drawing. By frequently practicing speed sketching, you will find yourself learning to ignore detail (because there is no time for detail in five minutes!) and to look at the main large shapes and angles.

In this sketch of a street scene, I established the street with an angled line and a curved line. I used an angled line to establish the top of the arches, and another to indicate the buildings on the street. I added in a few vertical lines as well as a few arches. One trick that I use to draw people walking is to find a place, for example a café, where people are walking toward me or away from me. As they walk near me, I can quickly get a few lines down.

When trying to teach yourself to only put down the main lines, it is sometimes helpful to use a pen to draw. This forces you to try to achieve better accuracy because you know you can't erase it.

In this water scene, I quickly captured the large shapes of the land formations without paying attention to detail. I used the side of my pencil to add some tone to the big value shapes. For the light-valued rock formations, I used a slightly scribbly motion to indicate some texture. For the water, I used horizontal strokes smeared with some facial tissue.

When you want to get values down quickly, it is best to use a soft pencil. These pencils offer flexibility and will cover the page more efficiently.

USING BASIC SHAPES

Daffodils, although very pretty, can be a challenge to draw. When drawing any complex subject, the easiest way to get started is to observe its basic shapes. Just look for the simplest shapes that can represent the object—in this case, you can think of the center part of the flower as a cup shape, and simplify the petals into one large geometric shape.

◄ **Step 1** I begin by first evaluating how tall the flowers are in relation to the width. I also study the angles of the stems and the position and direction of the cups of the flowers. I block in the stems, cups, and petals by blocking in the shapes with straight lines and ovals.

Blocking in with Shapes

The most important shortcut in drawing is to simplify your subject by using basic shapes and lines to block it in. The first step is learning to ignore the many wonderful details of your subject. Try imagining the largest, most basic shapes and lines to represent the size and position of your subject. There's no right or wrong way to do this—here, I've demonstrated three ways you could block in a banana.

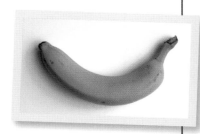

Here I use a simple crescent shape to represent the banana.

You can also block in a subject with straight lines.

You'll probably get the best results by using a combination of shapes and lines to represent your subject.

◄ **Step 2** Now that I have established the basic shapes of the daffodils, it is much easier for me to draw the petals. I ignore the details and focus on drawing the main shape of each one. I add a few curves to the cups and a few lines to indicate the main petals of the bud.

▶ **Step 3** Now I place a piece of heavyweight tracing paper over the drawing, taping it down with artist's drafting tape so that it doesn't shift. I use the drawing underneath as my guide, and begin to redraw the flowers. This time, however, I use a more refined contour. I carefully study the many delicate cup folds of the flower. I start adding some details to the petals and the bud, ignoring the initial block-in lines. I also redraw the stems and leaves. When I am satisfied with the drawing, I transfer it to a clean piece of plate-finish Bristol paper.

Shading to Follow Forms

To help increase the illusion of dimension, shade with strokes that follow the form. In this example, you can see how just the direction of the strokes used can make a big difference.

1. Here I shaded the ribbon with straight parallel horizontal strokes, without consideration to the contours, or the direction of the fold of the ribbon.

2. Here I used vertical parallel strokes without consideration of the form.

3. Finally, I used parallel strokes that follow the form of the ribbon. Even though I have not used any light and shadow patterns, the ribbon appears to be more three-dimensional.

Step 4 Using the side of a 2B pencil, I now lay in the base tone of the flowers. With long strokes, I follow the direction of the forms. I also work on the petals and cups, using light strokes that follow the curve and direction of the forms. Next I shade the insides of the cups and buds, using heavier pressure to produce a darker tone.

Step 5 To deepen the tone of the stems and leaves, I alternate between using the side and the dull point of a 4B pencil, creating long strokes. Switching back to the 2B pencil, I delicately shade the petals, using strokes that follow their curves. I then shade the insides and outsides of the cups, deepening the tones in the shadow areas. For the bud, I use light curved strokes that follow its egg-like form, and shorter strokes with heavy pressure to add tone to its inside.

Step 6 I use a sharp HB pencil to refine the shading of the flowers and the stems, following the direction of the forms before using a kneaded eraser to pick out the highlights. As a last touch, I lightly blend a few areas along the stems with a clean stump. Once I am satisfied, I clean up the drawing paper with a kneaded eraser and protect it with a sheet of tracing paper until I am ready to frame it.

SKETCHING A STILL LIFE

You don't need an elaborate setup to create a beautiful drawing—artists throughout the ages have created great artwork using everyday objects as their subject matter. You can find inspiration for a still-life setup virtually anywhere: your desktop, your nightstand, or even your breakfast table!

◀ Look for colorful objects of various sizes and textures to create an interesting still life. A single source of natural light is best, so I placed the setup by a window, moving the items around until I found a well-balanced composition.

▼ **Step 1** I start the drawing on heavyweight tracing paper and begin by observing the height and width of the composition and where the objects are positioned within it. I lightly block in the basic shapes of the objects. To help judge the symmetry of my shapes, I draw vertical lines down the center of the ellipses.

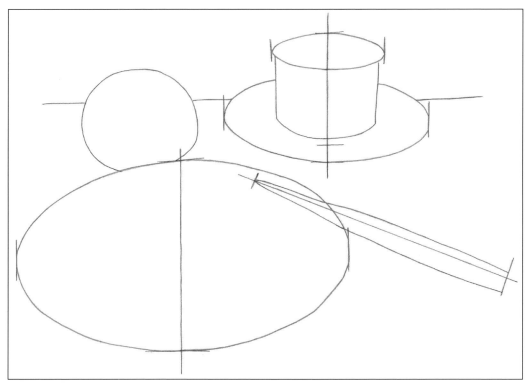

Step 2 Next I take another piece of heavyweight tracing paper and tape it on top of the drawing. I redraw the main elements of the still life, and then I add the curved shape of the orange peel, the crescent of the croissant, and the smaller berries.

Drawing Round Objects

A still life is great practice for developing your skill in representing round objects.

There are two great tricks to making edges appear more round: using reflected light in the shadow area (A), and using slightly darker shading in the light areas closest to the edges (B). Remember that a cast shadow helps "ground" the object. Cast shadows are always darkest near the form (C), and the edges become more diffuse as it gets farther away from the object (D).

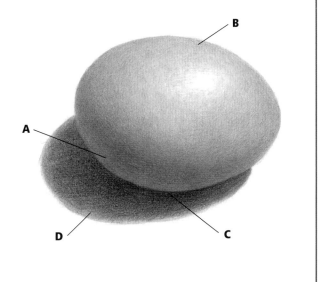

Step 3 Now I take a new piece of heavyweight vellum and trace over this drawing. This time I carefully redraw it, using the previous drawing as my guide. I refine the shapes, and start adding some details. When I'm satisfied that I've captured the details accurately, I transfer the drawing to a clean piece of plate-finish Bristol paper.

Tip! *Ellipses are a standard in almost any still life drawing, so you want to be sure you can draw them accurately. You can use a template if you like, but this is another way to ensure accuracy if you draw them freehand.*

Shape

The ellipse at left is correct; the one in the middle is too flat, while the one on the right is too pointed.

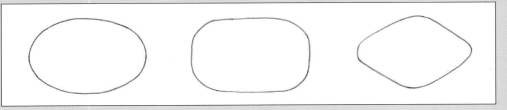

Step 4 Next I want to quickly establish a base tone, indicating the major values of the still life. I use a stump to add a dark layer of graphite to the deepest values of the objects, using strokes that follow the shapes. I move from the darker tones to the lighter ones, without adding any more graphite. I also use the stump to establish the texture of the objects. I use small circular strokes for the orange, longer irregular strokes for the croissant, and small, circular strokes with the tip of the stump for the berries.

Symmetry

It's easy to check the symmetry of your ellipse with a piece of tracing paper.

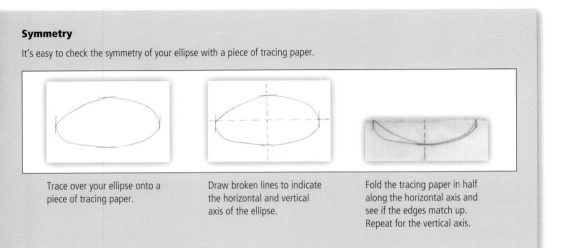

Trace over your ellipse onto a piece of tracing paper.

Draw broken lines to indicate the horizontal and vertical axis of the ellipse.

Fold the tracing paper in half along the horizontal axis and see if the edges match up. Repeat for the vertical axis.

Step 5 Now that the values are established, I use my pencils to shade the objects. I use heavier strokes and pressure for the darkest areas, and lighter strokes, lighter pressure, and pencil points for the lighter areas. I always create strokes that follow the shapes of the objects. Then I use a kneaded eraser to lift out highlights.

Details

Step 6 Now I use a stump to lightly smear some tone into the lightest areas. To create more texture on the orange peel, I add some irregular dots (also called stippling). Once the tones of the still life are brought to the correct values, I go over the drawing with an HB pencil, refining the shading where necessary.

Details

COMBINING REFERENCES

Drawing from photos is an easy way to choose your next subject—but sometimes it's difficult to find the perfect shot. For an easy fix, choose elements from more than one photo to create your own perfect shot. For this portrait of a chipmunk, I combined two photos: one with a pose I liked, and another with the background I preferred.

Step 1 I begin with two basic oval shapes to represent his head and body, and a curved shape to represent his arms. I add smaller oval shapes for the hands, ears, and eye, and I add another shape to represent the peanut. Then I draw the basic shape of the rock.

Step 2 I take a new piece of heavyweight tracing paper and tape it to my first drawing. I then begin to redraw the chipmunk. I refine the shape of his head and body, and I carefully draw his eyes, nose, ears, and mouth. I then draw his hands and feet, as well as the peanut. I draw the tail, curving it slightly to add more interest to the drawing. Around the edges of his body, I use short lines to indicate fur. I add the stripes and then draw the rock. When finished, I transfer the drawing to a clean piece of plate-finish Bristol paper.

Step 3 Using a new piece of heavyweight tracing paper, I trace over the main outlines of the chipmunk and rock. I carefully cut it out of the tracing paper and place it exactly over the shape of the chipmunk and rock on my drawing, so that it will act as a mask. I tape this to the drawing at the bottom to keep it in place and work on my dark background (see box below).

Creating a Dark Background Quickly

Dark backgrounds can add impact or drama to your drawing, but can take a lot of time if you use your pencil. With tracing paper as a mask to protect the main subject of your drawing, you can quickly add a dark background with carbon pencils, graphite powder, charcoal, or watercolor.

I use artist's drafting tape to line the edge of the drawing to create a clean edge.

Then I then dip a chamois cloth in graphite powder to quickly add tone to the background, using the finger of my other hand to hold the mask down and taking care not to smudge the paper. I can repeat this process as many times as I like, deepening the tone each time. When the tone is dark enough, I lift up the mask and carefully clean any smears with a kneaded eraser.

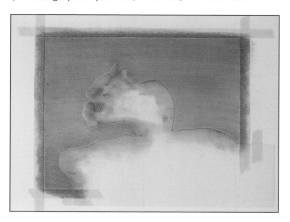

Step 4 I keep tracing paper under my hand as I draw to prevent the background from smearing. I use my kneaded eraser and stump to soften the hard edge of the mask, and then I use a stump to add some base tone to the darker areas of the fur, ears, and eyes. I use the side of a 2B pencil on the chipmunk, using short strokes to establish the direction of the fur. I use heavier pressure to draw in the stripes of his fur and use a sharp 4B to shade the dark value of the eye, leaving the highlight area white. I then use a sharp HB around his hands and feet. I use the stump to add tone to the peanut and use the side of a 6B to create a base tone of rough texture for the rock.

Tip!

To avoid smearing your drawing, some artists use a mahlstick, which is a wooden stick with a rubber tip that can be found at art supply stores. Place the rubber end of the mahlstick on the drawing support (not the drawing paper) and lean your hand on the stick so your hand does not touch or smear the drawing.

Step 5 To help avoid smearing the background, I work from the top down. I alternate between using the side and point of a 2B, and the point of an HB to create the fur texture, building it up with short strokes. For the stripes, I add a dark layer of tone with the point of a 6B pencil. I use a sharp HB to define the eyes, and then I deepen them with both the 4B and HB pencils. I shade the inside of the ears with a 2B and 4B, and I use a sharp HB to develop the hands and feet. I model the peanut, alternating between the stump and the 2B and HB pencils.

Taking a Second Look

After spending many hours looking at your drawing, it can be hard to see mistakes. Try these tricks to see your drawing with fresh eyes:

- Look at your drawing in a mirror. I keep a hand mirror near my drawing table just for this purpose.
- Try turning your drawing upside down. If you are working from a photo, you can also look at the photo upside-down for a comparison.
- Look at your drawing in dim light. This is particularly helpful for checking your shading.

Step 6 Now I build up the texture of the fur on the tail with longer strokes, and I use a very sharp 4B to draw hairs that overlap into the background. I also use a kneaded eraser to pick out some light areas of the fur. I establish more texture on the rock very quickly by alternating between the side of my 6B pencil and stump. When I am done with the final details, I clean the edges of the drawing and cover it with tracing paper until I am ready to spray it with fixative and frame it.

Details

DRAWING WITH A GRID

When creating a drawing where precision is necessary, a grid makes the job much faster and easier. Not only does a grid speed up the drawing process, but it also helps develop and improve eye-hand coordination, which is the foundation of all drawing.

Because grids can be used for many different projects, I like to have two on hand: a digital one that resides in my computer, and one that is printed or drawn with a ruler and ink on acetate.

Step 1 I tape the acetate grid over my photo and print out a blank grid on plain paper. Then I use a sharp HB pencil to lightly draw in the main outlines of the dog, ignoring the details. The secret to drawing with the grid is to concentrate on one box at a time, comparing it with the corresponding box of the photo. In this way, you forget about the subject you're drawing and focus instead on the lines in each box.

Step 2 I tape a piece of heavyweight tracing vellum over the drawing of the grid. Then I redraw the dog (not the grid lines), adding in her fur. I focus on the direction of hair growth, rather than being sure that each line is exactly the same as the photo. I add in some short lines around the face and close to the ears. Once I am satisfied with the accuracy of the drawing, I transfer it from the tracing paper to a new piece of plate-finish Bristol paper.

Using The Grid To Change Size

Renaissance artists once used the grid method as a way of enlarging their sketches to create magnificent murals, but you can also use it to reduce or enlarge any drawing.

For this example of a pear, I create three grids that are pro-portional to one another. The middle grid is the same size as the actual photo of the pear. The first grid is proportionately smaller, and the last grid is proportionately larger. Drawing one box at a time, I re-create the pear in each of the grids so that I end up with three different sized pears.

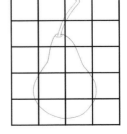

Step 3 Next I establish the shadow patterns on the fur. Using the side of a 2B pencil, I quickly stroke in tone, following the direction of the fur. For the ears, I use strokes that angle upward, referring frequently to the photo to be sure the direction of my strokes follow the direction of the fur. I lightly add some tone to establish a base layer for her eyes and mouth, and I use small circular strokes for her nose. For the hair around her neck, I use longer, curved strokes.

Drawing with an Eraser

When you have small, light areas in a drawing, such as highlights in fur texture or eyes, it is often easier to lift them out with a kneaded eraser instead of carefully drawing around them. My favorite tools for this technique are a kneaded eraser, a plastic eraser, and an eraser shield.

Here I kneaded the eraser into a point to create the left round marks. For the right long curved marks, I shaped the kneaded eraser so that is was long, flat and curved, and used the edge to lift out these shapes.

An eraser shield acts like a stencil, so you can easily lift out shapes with a plastic eraser.

Here I used a razor knife to cut a wedge-shaped edge on a plastic eraser. I then used the sharp edge of the eraser to create long, thin lines.

Step 4 I continue to work with the side of the 2B pencil, going back to the shadow areas to add another layer of tone. Working in the light areas of her head, I use short strokes and light pressure. I deepen the tone of her eyes with the side of the pencil, and then I dab the shaped point of a kneaded eraser to lift out the highlights. I refine the fur around her neck and add detail to her nose with small, circular strokes.

Step 5 Using the point and side of the 2B, I gradually build up texture and tone around the ears, focusing on the darker areas. I also use my kneaded eraser as a drawing tool, using the point I've shaped to lift out the lighter areas. Then I go back and lightly draw in the long hairs in the lighter areas. I use short strokes on the head to build up the hair texture. In the very light areas, I use an HB pencil instead, and then a kneaded eraser to lift out the highlight areas. I build up the tone on the nose with a 4B pencil and circular strokes, and then I lift out the highlight. Working on the eyes, I use heavy pressure on a 2B and 4B pencil. I use a stump very lightly to blend some of the tone in this area and a sharp 2B around the edges of the eye and eye highlight.

Tip!

Drawing Fur By Lifting Out

When I am drawing animals, using the lifting out technique makes the job much easier. It also has the added advantage of adding more texture to the fur.

Shape a kneaded eraser into a blunt rounded tip. Then "draw" the shape, lifting out the graphite.

Then go back in with a sharp HB pencil, drawing in the hairs with long strokes.

Step 6 As I get to the final stage of my drawing, I look at the drawing in a mirror to see where I need to add more tone. Then I refine and build up the hair texture with the point of an HB pencil. I sharpen some of the shadow areas, and as I work toward the bottom, I use long, straight strokes to "fade out" the fur. When I am satisfied that the drawing is completed, I clean the drawing of any smudges with a kneaded eraser.

SIMPLIFYING A SCENE

When you're looking for inspiration, don't be intimidated by a complex subject. A snapshot (like this one of Bow Bridge in New York City's Central Park) can make a wonderful drawing. Don't be afraid to simplify what you see—you don't need to render every single element to create a wonderful drawing that captures the essence of the scene.

◄ I cropped this wide shot to create a square format. I also decided to simplify the scene by leaving out the rowboats and the people on the bridge, so that the focus of the drawing would be the graceful architecture and the surrounding natural textures.

▼ **Step 1** I start by breaking down the big elements of the scene, blocking in the basic shapes and lines of the bridge, shoreline, and building. I divide the trees into three large masses, focusing on proportion and composition.

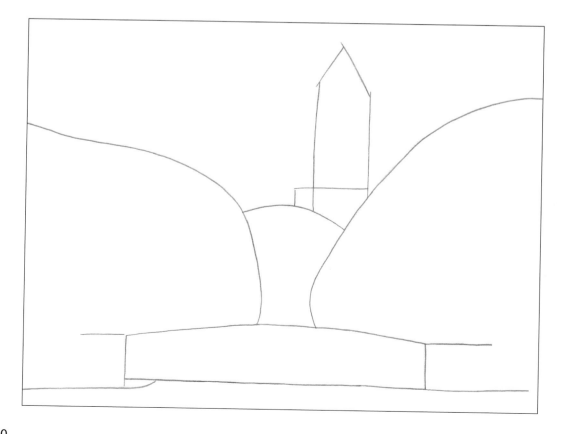

Step 2 I begin to break up the large tree areas into smaller masses. I also add a few lines to indicate the major branches. I add the arch under the bridge, carefully studying the shape of the curve, although I'm not worried at this point about it being perfect. Then I add some lines to indicate the main shapes within the building.

Using Templates

When drawing architectural subjects, artists frequently rely on tools to help speed up the process, as well as to increase the accuracy of the lines. In this photo, you can see some of the typical aides that have been used by artists over the years. Many contemporary artists use computers to improve their drawings as well.

- Template: helpful for drawing windows, portals, and small buildings
- French Curve Template: helpful for drawing curves and ellipses
- Triangle: Indispensable for drawing perfectly straight lines
- Flexible Ruler: Bendable into any shape, it's perfect for long, smooth curves

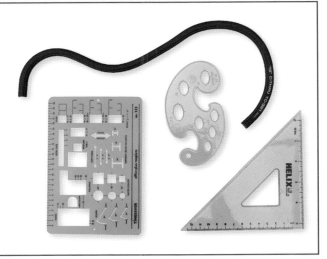

Step 3 Next I tape a piece of heavyweight tracing vellum over the drawing and begin to redraw with more accuracy and detail. I use my drawing tools to sketch the building, and then I break up the trees into smaller masses, adding more detail to each. Next I use a flexible ruler to create the long, curved lines of the bridge. Then I add some horizontal lines to indicate the main values in the water. I can now transfer the drawing to a clean piece of plate-finish Bristol paper.

Tip! *When you don't have time to shade every single rock or ripple of water, try using one of these techniques.*

Quick and Easy Rocks

Textured paper, such as cold press, can help create the texture of your subject. With a few light strokes of a soft pencil's side, the paper will pick up the graphite unevenly and create a rocky texture. Just add a few details with a sharp pencil, and you've got rocks!

Step 4 When I want to speed up the process in a landscape, I use a large stump dipped in graphite powder to lay in a base tone. I apply it to the tree area, using irregular circular strokes. Working quickly, I add darker tone to the main shadow areas of the trees. With just a little graphite left on the stump, I stroke some light tone into the sky. I add more powder to the stump, and I tone the shadow side of the building. I also use some dark tone to shade the underside of the bridge, and I add some very light tone to its front plane. Then I add tone to the water using horizontal strokes.

Quick and Easy Water

Calm water is best rendered with plate-finish paper. For rougher water, use a rougher paper, such as cold press. Use loose, horizontal strokes and vary the pressure to quickly render water. Lift out highlights with a kneaded eraser.

Step 5 Next I even out the light tone of the sky, using horizontal strokes and very light pressure with an HB pencil. I use the same pencil to shade the building and add some details to the bridge. For the trees, I use the side of a 6B pencil and irregular strokes, applying more pressure in the shadow areas. I switch to a 2B pencil to apply long horizontal strokes across the water.

Step 6 To add more texture to the trees, I use a 2B pencil and a short, uneven strokes. With a kneaded eraser, I dab and lift out some of the lighter areas in the leaves. Then I use a sharp 4B pencil to indicate the branches. I use crosshatching strokes to add more tone to the building. To create the texture of the shrubbery along the shore, I make short, vertical strokes with a dull 4B, using heavier pressure to create shadows. I then continue to build up tone in the water with the sides and point of several different pencils, using horizontal strokes. I lift out the final highlights with a kneaded eraser and step back to survey my work.

DEPICTING DISTANCE

The illusion of depth can be challenging to render on a two-dimensional page. But it's easier than you think—and a landscape is a quick way to learn how to create realistic drawings that seem three-dimensional.

▶ This scene shows a fairly clear delineation between foreground (the trees, grass, and wildflowers at the front of the photo), the middle ground (the homes and hills in the center of the photo), and the mountains and clouds in the distance.

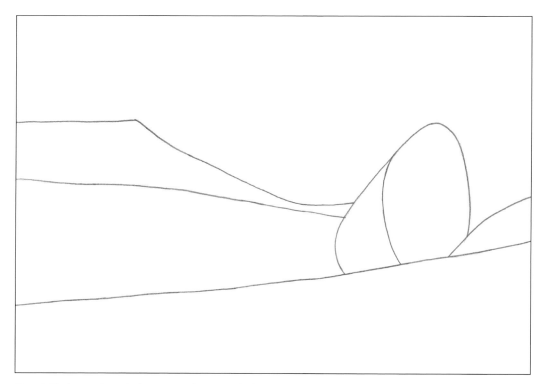

Step 1 The largest shapes in this scene are the trees in the foreground, so I first establish the foreground line and sketch the tree mass as an egg shape. I draw a line to delineate the middle ground area, and then I draw another line to block in the mountain mass. Before I go any further, I check that the proportions of these areas are correct.

Step 2 Next I block in two more oval shapes to depict the other tree masses in the foreground. I add two more lines to break up the middle ground shape, which represent tree lines. Then I add another mountain mass in the background and draw the main shapes of the clouds.

Drawing Clouds
Clouds are quick and easy to draw in three simple steps.

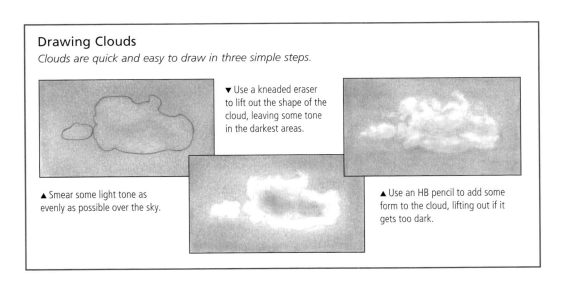

▼ Use a kneaded eraser to lift out the shape of the cloud, leaving some tone in the darkest areas.

▲ Smear some light tone as evenly as possible over the sky.

▲ Use an HB pencil to add some form to the cloud, lifting out if it gets too dark.

Step 3 Now I take a piece of heavyweight tracing vellum and tape it to my initial sketch. I redraw the foreground line and tree masses, using a more natural irregular line. I add some lines to indicate the major tree branches, and then I draw in the shapes of the trees in the middle ground. I add more detail to the mountains and clouds, and when I am satisfied that my drawing is accurate, I transfer the drawing to vellum Bristol paper.

Creating Depth

Creating a sense of depth in a landscape is not as difficult as you may think.

- Use more contrast of tone in the foreground and less contrast as the landscape recedes.
- Use more detail in the foreground, and less detail in the background.
- Overlap objects—for example, use a tree in the foreground that overlaps the middle ground and background.

This quick sketch illustrates all three rules: the foreground tree is darkest and most detailed, and it overlaps the middle ground and background.

Step 4 I quickly add a base tone using a stump and graphite powder. By working quickly, I create more irregular strokes, which translate into a more natural base tone. For the grass in the foreground, I use long, vertical, irregular strokes. I use darker tone and irregular circular strokes for the trees. To add tone to the mountains, I use lighter pressure with choppy strokes that change direction. I use the leftover graphite on the stump to lightly shade the sky with horizontal strokes.

Step 5 The texture of the paper is doing a lot of the work for me, so this next step goes very quickly. In the foreground, I add long, slightly curved strokes for the grass. Using a soft 6B pencil, I use a squiggly stroke to add texture to the trees, adding pressure in the shadows. For the details on the mountains, I switch to a 2B pencil and make choppy strokes that change direction. To create highlights in the snow and clouds, I use a kneaded eraser and lift out the graphite. Then I use the side of an HB pencil and a stump to even out the tone in the sky.

Tree Textures

Drawing every leaf on a tree would be painstakingly time consuming. It's much quicker to represent leaves with texture. Using a base wash with graphite powder and a stump can speed up the process too, especially if you start with rough or cold-pressed paper.

Here you can see how different types of strokes are rendered on rough and smooth papers; you can choose your preference depending on how much time you have and how much detail you want to include.

Smooth

Rough

Short strokes create a nice texture for evergreen trees.

Irregular, scribbly strokes work well for deciduous trees.

Short, U-shaped strokes can also be used for deciduous trees.

Step 6 Working from background to foreground, I add the final details and touch up everything. First, I use light pressure to add the wildflowers. Then I use sharp, hard pencils for the finest details, and soft, large pencils for the rest. Where I need the lightest highlights, I use a kneaded eraser to lift them out. I compare my drawing to the photo and am satisfied with the rendering.

Tip!

If you don't have panoramic landscape photos of your own to draw from, look to other sources of inspiration—postcards, calendars, or magazine ads can all work. Or try searching for images of some of your favorite locales online.

SKETCHING A PORTRAIT

Probably one of the most difficult challenges in art is to capture a person's likeness in a portrait. The slightest inaccuracy in the drawn lines of a lip or an eye can make the drawing seem "not quite right." One of the best shortcuts for helping the artist draw more accurate lines is to use a grid. By focusing on each small box of the grid, and forgetting that you are drawing a person, you will find how quickly and easily you can create a likeness.

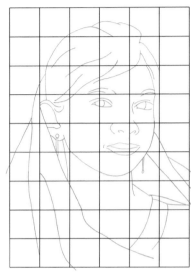

Step 1 I place a grid over my portrait photo and begin, drawing only the main lines in each box. Because this is the foundation of the drawing, I have found that the best "shortcut" to capturing a realistic likeness is to go slowly and surely so that the lines are accurately drawn.

Step 2 I take a piece of heavyweight tracing vellum and trace and redraw the lines without the grid, capturing the nuances of the lines. As I draw, I refine the lines and double and triple check the accuracy of each line, angle, and curve. Once I am satisfied with the drawing, I transfer it to a piece of plate-finish Bristol paper and clean-up any smudges with a kneaded eraser.

Step 3 Next I study the shadow patterns on her face and hair. I note that both her hair and eyes are very dark, so I want to establish them at the earliest stage of the shading. I use a 2B on the hair, drawing long strokes with the side of the pencil that follow the direction of hair growth. I then apply a dark tone to her eyes and eyebrows and to the deep shadow of the sari, using long strokes that follow the direction of the folds. Next I add shading to the face, using light pressure with the side of the 2B and following the contours of her face.

Step 4 Now I work on developing the base tones of the portrait. I use the side of a 4B to darken the shadows of the hair, and then switch to the point of the 4B to draw long, curved lines that follow the direction of the strands. I use heavy pressure to deepen the dark tone of the sari behind her neck, and then I use a 2B to deepen the shading of her eyes, using both circular and radial strokes but leaving the highlight area white. To build up the shading of the face, I continue to use strokes that follow the contours of her features. For the pattern on the sari, I use an eraser to lift out the light shapes.

Drawing Hair

The key to drawing natural looking hair is to think about the mass of the hair as well as the direction of hair growth and not the many thousands of individual hairs. By shading the masses of the hair with strokes that follow the direction of hair growth, the hair texture will develop naturally.

Draw the main shapes of the waves of hair and add just a few lines to indicate the direction of hair growth with an HB pencil.

Use the side of a 2B pencil to shade the dark side of the waves of hair. Use long strokes that curve and follow the direction of hair growth.

Build up the tone with the side of the 2B pencil, using heavier pressure on the shadow side and lighter pressure on the light side of the waves. Then use the point of a kneaded eraser to lift out some highlights.

Step 5   I always begin a drawing by shading very lightly so that I can make corrections to my shading as I go without much erasing. But at this point I feel confident that I understand the forms of her face, so I begin to add deeper tones of shading with heavier pressure. Then I use an HB to begin adding light shading to the light side of the forms. I also use the HB to refine the shading in the eyes, being mindful of the spherical shape of the eyeball as I lightly work on the whites. I use the point of a

Step 6 In this step, I return to using the 4B pencil to build up the texture of the hair. I use both the side and the point of the pencil, always following the direction of the hair. I also develop the dark shadows of the sari with the 4B, using the point of an HB to refine the edges of these shadows. Continuing to work with the HB, I build up the tone on the light side of the face, always following the contours of the features. I then work in the shadow side, building up with the HB to refine the shading. I use the pencil's point to carefully refine the shapes of the features. I add detail to the earrings with the HB and draw in a few individual strands of hair around the forehead.

Creating the Illusion of Roundness

When drawing the human form, artists throughout the ages have used a simple trick to help create the illusion of round-ness of form by adding an accessory. For example, in a portrait, an artist may add a necklace or a bracelet to help the neck or the arm of the subject appear more round.

In this example, I drew the outline of the lower part of an arm. In the drawing on the immediate left, I added a simple bracelet. You can see here how the bracelet adds a third dimension to an otherwise two-dimensional drawing.

Step 7 I like to call this step the "polishing" stage of the portrait. This is when I carefully rework the shading of the face, lightly using the point of the HB to fill in uneven areas, and using the kneaded eraser to lightly lift out tone that is too dark. I finish the portrait by adding more shading to the sari with light crosshatching strokes. When I'm done, I clean up any remaining smudges with a kneaded eraser and place a piece of tracing paper over the drawing to protect it until I'm ready to frame it.

OUTLINING TO SAVE TIME

One timesaver that artists often rely on to create complex drawings is to trace the outline of the subject. Even artists such as Norman Rockwell and Jan Vermeer have used this technique to start their drawings. Try not to rely too much on this method, however, because although it a great timesaver, it does not help develop your artistic eye as effectively.

Step 1 I begin with an enlarged photo that is the same size as my tracing and drawing papers. Before I begin to trace, I study the photo I have chosen, looking for the most important lines to trace. I place a piece of heavyweight tracing vellum over the photo and begin to trace these lines. When I'm done, I compare the tracing to the photo to be sure that I have enough for a good start on the drawing. Then I transfer this tracing to a clean piece of plate-finish Bristol paper.

Hand Sketches

Hands are difficult to draw for many artists, but the easiest way to start learning to draw them is to do a lot of quick hand sketches. When you are drawing hands, look for the big shapes and block in the masses, using lines to help you see the angles. I also like to use curved lines when drawing hands to indicate the position of the small joints of the fingers, as well as the fingertips. For practice, try taking some quick photos of your own hands and practice sketching them from your photos.

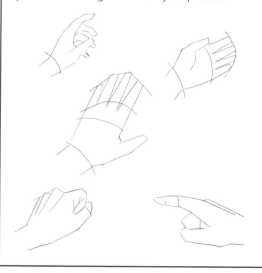

Muscles Create Form

When you are drawing the human body, it is important to remember that the under-lying muscles create most of the forms. Muscles always have a "belly" in the center, which causes the human form to have a series of convex shapes. There are very few concave lines in the human body. If you keep this simple idea in mind when you draw the human body, your portraits will look more realistic.

Here you can see the "belly" of the muscle.

Using convex lines to draw form, the correct way.

Using concave lines to draw form is a common mistake.

Step 2 I start to establish a base tone for the shadows and dark values by using the side of a 2B pencil to lay down a layer of tone in the hair. I also add dark tone to the eyebrows, lips, and nostrils. Using lighter pressure, I add shading to the delicate shadow areas of the face, neck, and body. As always, I draw using strokes that follow the form. Because the dress is semi-transparent, I add some light tone to indicate the form of her legs, which can be partially seen through the material. Then I add some light tone to the dress using long, vertical strokes.

Quick and Easy Lips

When light is coming from above, the parts of the form that are facing up receive the light. In contrast, the parts of the form that face down are in shadow. This concept helps simplify shading.

First, add tone to the down plane of the lips (the upper part of the lip that faces down).

Add additional tone to the upper lip, and then add some very light tone to the lower lip, which is the plane of the lips that faces up. Leave the highlight area white.

Use the point of a kneaded eraser to lift out the outline of the lips. Deepen the shading of the upper lip and add some tone around the areas where the lips meet. Add more shading to the lower lip, being sure to maintain the contrast between the upper and lower areas.

Step 3   I go back to drawing the hair, using the dull point of a 4B pencil and following the direction of hair growth. Using a 2B, I add more tone to the shadow side of the face, noting that the light falls most directly on the side. I work around the body, adding more tone to areas where the forms turn away from the main light source. I add more shading to the upper part of the dress, again using strokes that follow the form of the body. I loosely add more long lines to indicate the folds of the dress, and then I add more tone to the shoes.

Step 4 I now work with an HB pencil and begin to add tone in the light areas. I work around her face, carefully shading her features with curved strokes that follow her form. I do the same around the neck area, shading the forms that indicate the underlying muscles of the neck. I continue to work around her arms and chest area, and begin to develop the shading on her hands. As I work

Step 5 I return to working on her hair using the side of a 4B to achieve deeper tones, working softly around the hairline. I then use a sharp 2B to add a few lines to indicate some additional texture. I use the HB to delicately shade the flowers in her hair. Next I work on refining the shading of the tones on her face and body, using mainly the HB pencil. In some of the deeper shadow areas,

Step 6 After checking my drawing in the mirror to spot any inaccuracies, I work on a few final details. I examine the folds of the dress, and decide to deepen the shading with long, vertical strokes. I don't try to draw each fold exactly; instead I work to get their texture, working loosely and quickly. I then add some additional shading to the shoes. As a final touch, I draw light horizontal lines across the bottom of the drawing to ground the dancer. Finally, I clean up any smudges and am now ready to frame the drawing.

FINAL THOUGHTS

Developing a beautiful drawing takes lots of time, skill, and patience. But that doesn't mean you should shy away from using some techniques and shortcuts to help speed up the process. In this book I have shown you some of the tricks that I have developed or learned from other artists. As you practice and incorporate some of the techniques into your own drawings, I am confident you will also develop some of your own special ways to streamline your drawings. The key to developing some of your own individual shortcuts is to constantly sketch and experiment with your pencil and paper. Also, if you make a daily habit of sketching, you will find that your drawing ability and speed will increase by leaps and bounds, which will become the greatest shortcut of all. Enjoy!